MW00774381

SWEDISH DEATH CLEANING

How to Free Yourself From A Lifetime of Stuff

LINNÈA GUSTAFSSON

TABLE OF CONTENTS

INTRODUCTION

Every single day you keep adding weight to the heavy pack on your back. Wearing a backpack loaded with bricks is the perfect image to describe how most people feel. We all know how it goes. Your house is full of things you either bought yourself, you got gifted or you inherited because you thought one day you might need it, And yet, the canvas you once bought with the intention to fill your free time with more creative tasks remains empty.

The older we get; the more clutter we accumulate. Every single day you keep adding weight to the heavy pack on your back. We all know how it goes. Your house is full of things you either bought yourself, you got gifted or you inherited because you thought one day you might need it. And yet, the canvas you once bought with the intention to fill your free time with more creative tasks remains empty. The older we get, the more clutter we accumulate.

In "Swedish Death Cleaning", you'll discover:

- A day-by-day guide to clean up your life in 4 days

- 3 most important types of tidying up your life

- How to overcome denial and face the inevitable truth?

- The right mindset to avoid emotional stress and overcome your fears

- Practical exercises and the right questions to ask while decluttering

Now, It's time to do a simple transition to a minimal lifestyle by Swedish life style.

CHAPTER 1

WHAT IS DEATH CLEANING?

Death cleaning, as we know it today, is derived from the Swedish word, döstädning'. The word is the combination of 'dö' which translates to death, while 'städning' translates to cleaning. Therefore, death cleaning is a very literal translation of a term that, as we have previously stated, isn't as much about dying as it is about living.

Death cleaning has been described as a 'Swedish phenomenon', a process through which the elderly and their families 'set their affairs in order'. However, it is worthy of mention that more people than those in the senior citizen demographic can benefit from this process. Every other adult who can comprehend this process can try their hands at death cleaning.

Death cleaning helps in the disposal of things you have bought, inherited, gifted or otherwise acquired that you don't need and might never use. Having the courage to let them go or even talk about them as a form of preparation is a huge component of the Swedish death cleaning culture.

There are multiple approaches to death cleaning and they are all based on the individual choices of the people practicing it. The proper time to begin death cleaning, as well as how long it should take, how to dispose and other considerations is not an exact science bound by rigid rules. Instead, the preferences of the people involved are what determines how the cleaning will be carried out.

Death cleaning can be practiced at any age or stage, whether dying or not since it is a very practical and useful activity. The process, in fact, is so practical, it helps you organize your life directly or indirectly. While some may argue that you can organize your life without "preparing" for death or "welcoming" it, the truth is people hardly organize themselves properly and even when they do, it's never for a considerable length of time. With issues like procrastination or lack of enthusiasm, efforts at organization can stop at anytime. However in the case of death cleaning, the individual involved is likely to organize their possessions as well as they can, especially when they consider the finality of the cause they have at heart.

How well have you lived your life? If you dropped dead today, how do you think people will remember you? If you aspire to regular values like the rest of us, then having your loved ones remember you in a good light after you pass on is probably important to you. It is perfectly natural for you to want your family, friends and loved ones to remember you as an organized person, who was also thoughtful and wise while they were alive. This is a particularly powerful impression which can remain in their minds forever. If you would like to achieve this, then you should definitely consider the practice of death cleaning.

In addition, if you are considering passing your belongings down on to your loved ones, you may want to consider a rethink. In today's times, people are not really keen on inheriting furniture, family heirlooms or any other vestiges of the past generation. This is mostly because trends appear every day and in such a fast-paced world, inherited property can quickly become a burden. Therefore, keeping only essential things will cause your loved ones to remember you as a person who was abreast of the times.

While we might have established that death cleaning is not as dreadful and gloomy a process as it sounds, it is still not a walk in the park. There could be multiple hiccups along the way since it entails a lot of courage, emotion and time.

CHAPTER 2

WHY DEATH CLEANING?

In present times, a lot of people desire that their lives be reflected in everything they do or touch. This means that we would all be thrilled if every item we touched gave off a reflection of our core personalities. We also want this core personality to shine through even after we are gone, such that when people remember us, they can feel the essence of our being and understand how we lived our lives.

It may not be a particularly pleasant fact that one day we will all cease to exist but since we know this to be a fact, it is never a bad thing to be prepared for the inevitable as opposed to being in perpetual denial.

Everyone you know – including yourself – is on the clock due to the inevitability of death, for death makes life meaningful. You should see this as a simple law of nature and acceptance of the fact that there is no life without death will spur you to stop procrastinating and act while you have the opportunity.

Death cleaning opens the doors to so many benefits in our lives. Preparation to live properly after the knowledge of an eventual transition can lead to a more focused lifestyle as well as a tidy home. Everyone, regardless of nationality, can learn from the Swedish people and follow their example of using the inevitability of death to organize and tidy up their lives.

CHAPTER 3

TYPES OF DEATH CLEANING

Since Death cleaning goes beyond "waiting to die", it follows that there will be multiple aspects to it. It is helpful to systematically categorize these aspects into groups that will be handled separately. This is because tossing every aspect of your life onto one huge pile, and roughly attempting to death clean them will be counter-productive; it will pose a challenge so difficult, it may be impossible to surmount.

Just as all things in a person's life belong to different categories, when it comes to death cleaning, such a blueprint must also be adhered to. This is especially important because the obvious purpose of death cleaning is to take a proper look into every aspect of your life to be sure that all things that rightfully belong to you are taken into due consideration.

As such, the following are the different types of death cleaning:

PHYSICAL DEATH CLEANING

Physical death cleaning, as the name implies, is the arrangement and categorization of your physical possessions which includes all your material belongings piled or stored up in your house. This is the easiest aspect to take care of as it mostly includes the physical things you can see and touch in your house.

This aspect of death management is the core of death cleaning. The ideal situation is that when you are gone, you leave behind the smallest possible amounts of possessions for your loved ones so that they are easy to handle. In physical death cleaning, your focus is on your living space and all the items you own in it.

You should move around your house, sorting out and getting rid of things that are no longer useful as you come across them. Sort through all of the clothing in your closet and dispose any of them you do not wear regularly or you are no longer in need of. Better still, you can donate these clothes to a charity organization. If you have any books lying around, you can give them to people who are in need of them and the gesture will surely be highly appreciated.

It may take some time but be clear on what you need to keep and what you don't so that when you are done, whatever physical possessions are left will be easy to handle by your loved ones. This action is akin to taking out your own trash, and you are the only one who can properly determine what constitutes trash to you. It is a very good idea to repeat this process every now and then so that you don't cancel the gains you've made.

And herein lies a bonus in disguise: acknowledgement of eventual death, in addition to a deep appreciation for the frailty of life, could also avail you of a neat and orderly home.

DIGITAL DEATH CLEANING

Today, especially in developed nations, more people than you can imagine, heavily depend on the World Wide Web or Internet to conduct their daily activities. When people want to listen to the news, conduct business or entertain themselves, the first place they usually go to is the internet. Consequently, the lives of many citizens around the world have become digitalized as social media has intricately connected the world.

This has made the world a global village of sorts in the real sense of the word. It is now normal for people to have digital footprints and records. But what happens when the person passes away? These records remain there, visible for people to see but without getting updates and over time, they are an ominous reminder of death. In many ways, this is the expected outcome because only few people prepare for death and even these people seem to forget about their digital presence.

Usually, the family of a deceased would want to deactivate all their digital accounts but getting access to these accounts proves to be very difficult. Since there was no pre-planned method to erase or even to access the social account of the deceased, the family might find this to be a nagging pain.

If you wish that when you leave, your social media accounts be taken proper care of, then you need to have a plan. Deactivation of your accounts when you pass on cannot happen through wishful thinking but through a calculated chain of events. This is of utmost important because many social media companies themselves have no clear-cut plan for handling accounts when someone passes. The best bet is deactivation after a period of inactivity and this isn't a solution that fits perfectly.

To solve this dilemma, you should keep some record of every account you have be sure to let your family, loved ones, or trustees know all your accounts that exist online. Revealing the password to each account might not be necessary at the moment – not to mention frightening – and so there is another option. You can create a diary entry or memo pad that contains all the accounts and their respective passwords. Such a document can be stored at the post office, the lawyer's office or any other agreed location.

In the event of your passing, it will be considerably simpler and more straightforward for your loved ones to take care of your digital property.

In addition, you should put all your computer-based property together, including those that aren't online. It is a good idea to browse through your computer desktop and make it as tidy as possible. You can delete duplicate copies, old and outdated documents, and unnecessary bits and pieces of information that are bound to be all over the place.

You should also find a competent filing system for your computer stuff especially in anticipation of future emails and files that you are surely bound to acquire. If you handle digital death cleaning properly, your family will not have to stress themselves because your music, pictures, letters and other commercial items like sales pages and royalties can be taken care of with ease.

You might have some information online that you would prefer to deal with on your own. This might be information that is either very personal or that could cause harm to people around you. This is very normal and you should not shy away from it. You can deal with this information privately and literally get yourself in order.

Finally, none of this is abnormal. Digital death management is increasingly becoming more popular and acceptable as people are now realizing its significance. Some experts have predicted that in the near future, people will begin to hire digital death managers to clean up their social media accounts and online businesses as well as that of their loved ones.

FINANCIAL DEATH CLEANING

When a person dies, closing out their finances becomes hard work. The process for loved ones to get access to a deceased person's bank account is an uphill task and numerous checks and counter checks have to be carried out to even begin.

There are usually requirements to be met at the bank, documents to be presented in a court of competent jurisdiction, and other documents to be signed and sworn to. This process can be very time-consuming and strenuous on different levels.

The bigger the investments and financial situation left behind by the deceased, the harder it is to resolve the situation. For instance, if the deceased left behind estates or companies, loved ones or family members have to go from one organization to the other to provide each bank with documents that prove that the account holder is deceased so that they can be given authority to access the account.

In the event that the deceased used a bank that operates wholly online, loved ones and family members have to present a credit card report as well as other relevant documents in order to access the account.

You can simplify this process by leaving instructions with your lawyer or financial institution that detail who exactly should be in charge or have access to your accounts when you are gone. This simple act ensures that your administrator or whoever you put in charge (including your family and loved ones) will be granted access to your financial accounts with the least stress possible.

Unless you actually do not intend to let anyone have access to your money after your demise, it is a good practice to make your bank account details accessible to your designated administrator well ahead of your eventual death.

CHAPTER 4

THE OLD AND NEW ABOUT SWEDISH DEATH CLEANING

Up until about 2017, the phrase Swedish death cleaning wasn't really on anybody's lips or registering as a blip on somebody's radar. We, of course, have Magnusson to thank for the sudden rise of the catchphrase right on the heels of the KonMari method of decluttering and its own global spread. It's arguable, but Swedish death cleaning may have gained its popularity precisely because the "Spark Joy" movement had already paved the way for people to rethink the way they accumulate—in fact, hoard—their material possessions through the efforts of the Japanese tidying consultant, Marie Kondo.

According to an online article by Rachel Connor, a senior lecturer in Leeds Beckett University, Swedish death cleaning or dösstädning may have captured the fancy of the general populace because Scandinavian worldviews became a big deal right around that time. Connor reminded us of hygge, the Danish term for coziness, contentment, or well-being, which became a buzzword, starting the year before that, at least, in the publishing world. A cursory search on Amazon showed me the following books from 2016 and 2017: The Little Book of Hygge: Danish Secrets to Happy Living by Meik Wiking, How to Hygge: The Nordic Secrets to a Happy Life by Signe Johansen, and Hygge: The Danish Art of Happiness by Marie Tourell Søderberg, just to name three titles I chose randomly from the results.

It shouldn't come as a surprise to you that these books found an audience outside of their authors' stomping grounds and comfort zones. After all, since roughly around 2011, Denmark has consistently ranked among the top three happiest countries in the world. Surely, the secret to that much-coveted position (subjective as the global survey may be) was well worth sharing to the rest of humankind, which looked to the peoples of Northern Europe and its harsh geography and climate, for wisdom on how to live happy indeed. The milieu was just right. There were no barriers to entry for anything else hailing from that region. So when another Scandinavian emerged from the horizon with a fascinatingly morbid take on organizing homes and lives, people definitely paid attention. I certainly did myself. It was impeccable timing.

Let's also face one very important thing about the advance of Swedish death cleaning: It arrived on the scene, at the perfect moment, as a viable solution to a very real problem in the twenty-first century. It was confronting the issue of clutter. With prices of consumer goods plunging due to mass productions and the Black Friday sales of this world driving people bonkers for "stuff," overshadowing and throwing

Thanksgiving traditions out the window as people camped out of Walmarts or Targets or Best Buys almost immediately after cutting the holiday turducken, piles of junk and controlled confusion were bound to build up in homes and offices over the years.

My own personal hypothesis of its rise: the globalization of thought enterprises directly related to the cultures from which they came. People from across the Pacific Ocean buy into the KonMari method (especially now that Kondo has her own Netflix series, which launched in January 2019) because they relate its efficiency and simplicity to classic Japanese philosophies. Kondo herself mentioned it in an interview with Julia Brucculieri, published online in HuffPost, where she mentioned the Buddhist concept of wabi-sabi, "the art of finding beauty in the imperfect, impermanent, and incomplete." (Yes, I know Buddhism started in India, but the specific branch of Zen Buddhism associated to the KonMari method spread broadly in Japan and Korea, a mix of Indian Mahayana Buddhism and Chinese Taoism. That's a lot of cultural blending right there!)

When I was doing research on this book, I happened upon a friend married to a Dane, who had never heard about Swedish death cleaning. However, when I started explaining the concept to her, she pretty much said, "But of course. That's so Scandinavian." What she may have meant by that might be clarified as I tell you a bit more about the term.

The Swedish term dösstädning is a combination of two words, dö, which means "death" in English, and sstädning, which stands for "cleaning." Alone, each word seems innocuous enough, but when brought together, they are more than the sum of their parts. Contained in those eleven letters is the fundamental belief that it's a good idea to get rid of unnecessary things when you know you're about to buy a one-way ticket into oblivion. When that event looms large in front of you, you want to make sure that you're leaving your home and life in order. Far be it for your next of kin to have to worry about the logistics of telling Tindr-dom that you were done with hooking up with almost-total strangers for all eternity. It's not another person's responsibility. It's something you should take care of yourself. You certainly don't want to burden anybody else with your various entanglements.

While the initial motivation may be about readiness for death, in the end, Swedish death cleaning is about helping you live your best life by doing away with the very things that weigh you down. There's no point in clinging to stuff that means something only to you. If you do have items likely to make somebody else feel good, then exercising death cleaning means that you let go of them so that others may benefit from them in some measure. Instead of keeping things, give away your belongings to other people who are likely to appreciate them best. You win. They win. Everybody wins.

Can you now see why I'm doing my utmost to have you on board for the ride? Because there's a real value to you doing some death cleaning. Don't be spooked by the thought that you could be jinxing yourself and inviting death over to take you for a ride to your final destination. It's just simple and basic pragmatism on many levels. It's very likely that that's what my friend was thinking of when I told her about Swedish death cleaning.

Scandinavians (people from Denmark, Norway, and Sweden) are generally thought of as the quiet pragmatists. They are practical people. They survey their surroundings and find ways to adapt to what is there. They're not interested in stirring things up or overhauling systems. They're all about blending in and complementing the status quo, which was essentially what the Danish ambassador to Australia, Tom Nørring, said in a radio interview posted on the SBS website.

I can actually just call this whole decluttering philosophy "death cleaning," but I think attaching the adjective "Swedish" to it enhances its meaning. It doesn't just acknowledge the country from which Magnusson, initiator of its global popularity, hails, it also brings to the phrase the subtext of solid, unswerving practicality. I'm sure another book can do a study of its historical context going all the way back to the time of the Vikings and beyond, but for now, I just want to zero in on its current trend.

Swedish death cleaning is not about letting out your inner goth to focus on gloom and doom. It's about a literal and metaphorical abandonment of all encumbrances—unnecessary, unwanted, tired possessions and associations—that shouldn't be part of your life anymore. Perhaps different from the "spark joy" thinking of Kondo, this method of tidying up focuses more on an uncomplicated assessment of things and what to do with them afterward. Sure, that Rubik's cube might make you very happy because of the childhood memories it evokes, but after you pass away, no one else is going to want it or play with it. Everybody is staring down at their smartphones these days, looking to catch all the Pokémon they could find on their augmented-reality screens. So why keep the darn cube? A prominent feature of Swedish death cleaning is the throwaway box, which I'll discuss later in the book. It will serve as the final repository for that much-loved, but now impractical, block toy of yours.

While the KonMari method might focus on the here and now, the characteristic of presentness typical of the Japanese worldview, Swedish death cleaning considers today, yes, but also shuttles over to tomorrow and makes it a factor in your decision-making process for decluttering. When you take the future into your deliberations, it's now more than just emotional attachment that guides you. It helps you evaluate your life and how it may or may not affect the rest of the world, even if that simply means your immediate family, friends, and colleagues.

To recap, Swedish death cleaning is a concept of decluttering and tidying up that involves a pragmatic evaluation of your possessions and what to do with them in relation to your life today and in the future, when you're gone and other people, primarily your inner circle of loved ones, will have to deal with them and everything else that you leave behind. (Whew! That was a long sentence, but I wanted to get it all in one place for you to read and to think about.) You and I and the rest of humanity are all bound to die at some point. Death cleaning anticipates that by getting you ready at any time of your life so that you can carry on with real life and living. It's irrelevant if you have just one week or one century in your lifespan ahead of you. The essential thing to remember is that the cleaning philosophy provides you the tools to do away with things that don't matter and to concentrate instead on those that do.

If you dare plunge into it now, after all my gentle prodding, the good news for you is that Swedish death cleaning is not about decluttering in a hurry. You're not going to speed this up as just another item to tick off of your to-do list. It entails a process that could take a period of days to accomplish. After all, you don't really want to expedite something when it does have a bearing on your and others' eternity. Eve MacSweeney, in an online Vogue article, wrote that Swedish death cleaning is the slow-food version to organizing, and I tend to agree with her.

To close this chapter and move on to the next, let me quote directly from MacSweeney, so you can have a lot of things to think about. Hopefully, it is something that will get you engaged with the whole concept. "[Swedish death cleaning] is the steady acknowledgment and anticipation that you should start shedding the baggage of life rather than leave it for your unfortunate children to deal with. . . . It's also about facing one's eventual exit in a mature, healthy, and unsentimental way."

CHAPTER 5

WHY DECLUTTER?

I can go on and on about the many reasons why you should declutter but if you do not set personal goals towards decluttering, you are never going to get to do it. Worse still, you might carry it out without a purpose and end up with fresh accumulation and a newly cluttered home. This is why it is important to know why you should declutter.

Personalize your decluttering. Consider what you would achieve and what you would enjoy once your life and your home become organized. Once you can find ways in which decluttering is good for you, write them down as a reminder and refer to the list whenever you need some encouragement to help you stay organized.

Make the list handy and work towards achieving these goals.

Decluttering is good for you because it immediately reduces your stress and takes it away entirely in the long run. Clutter or more explicitly hoarding has been said to have the ability to derail your concentration. An unorganized home can make you restless and unable to focus on anything. It can also impact on your brain's ability to process information.

All these effects of clutter have been verified. A research at Princeton University for example says that staying unorganized and having a cluttered home can decrease your performance and increase your stress.

This is also the outcome of research undertaken by the UCLA's Center on Everyday Lives and Families (CELF) on 32 families. These families were shown to experience stress levels directly proportional with the things they owned in their homes. Thus, decluttering can increase your concentration and consequently your performance. It can also reduce stress and emotional baggage thereby causing you to live a more enjoyable life. If you ever need additional reasons to constantly declutter, you can always come back to check my reasons why clutter and hoarding is not good for you.

WHAT IS TRENDY?

Decluttering has been around for a long time. In fact, proponents have expressed it in various forms. However, they all point to the importance of living a simple life with fewer possessions. Some of the decluttering concepts in the 21st century include minimalism, hygge, dostadning and KonMari. These concepts have become something of a culture and trends that continue to re-emphasize themselves. The benefits they carry in helping us declutter and live more fulfilling lives are a pivotal reason they remain in vogue. We will now take a brief look at each one.

MINIMALISM

Minimalism is a decluttering concept that says that we should live with fewer things. Minimalists shred their possessions to the bare essentials but they do this with a view to attending towards their higher purpose. Minimalists feel that living with less is entering into freedom from the firm grip of material possessions. They posit that in our quest for accumulation, we forget those things that are important like our health and our family. Also, physical items that do nothing to promote our wellbeing should not take up all our space mentally, emotionally and physically.

However, the crux of minimalism is that you make decisions about the things you own consciously. Don't just go about buying everything you see. If you think that owning a lot of things helps you move towards your life goals then by all means you should own them. Minimalism only directs that we go about our acquisition with a conscious mind and a unity of purpose.

HYGGE

Hygge is a Danish word for "cozy" and a decluttering concept that proposes that you have more moments in your life that are special and trigger feelings of happiness, warmth and love. Hygge is not a specific set of activities to do but a consciousness that your life should not always be gloomy. Hygge is therefore much more a practice or a set of rituals that you have designed for yourself so that living life is more of an adventure. In this way, you can choose what gives you your hygge feeling.

DOSTADNING

Dostadning is the same as the Swedish death cleaning. It is a set of principles aimed to help you declutter your possessions and live with fewer so that if you pass away unexpectedly, your loved ones do not face a mass of clutter that are your belongings. Unlike hygge, dostadning proposes activities that culminate in having death cleaned and goes beyond finding happiness for you alone.

KONMARI

KonMari is a decluttering concept popularized by Japanese author Marie Kondo in her book, The Life-Changing Magic of Tidying Up. Although KonMari is a personal method that Kondo uses to stay organized, it carries very useful approaches to decluttering. To declutter using KonMari, you must be certain about which of your items spark joy for you. These are the only items you can keep. You can determine what sparks joy by the usefulness of the item or the memory they trigger.

When you declutter with the KonMari method, all the objects in your home would be things of immense value to you. No wonder, this decluttering concept like all the others have proven very valuable.

DAY ONE: UNDERSTANDING POSSESSION SELF EXTENSION

Today, we will participate in two activities. The first one has already been explained above and will help you get your organizing right. The second activity is a concept that will help you understand one of the two reasons you ended up with so much possessions in the first place. It is about your inability to let your possessions go because you see them as a part of you.

ACTIVITY ONE: YOUR PERSONAL DECLUTTERING GOALS

Step One: Get a journal and a pen.

It could be a book, a diary or just paper. Make sure it is something you will not misplace. If you are using paper, you may want to use clips to hold it in between a file.

Step Two: Find somewhere quiet to sit.

You can choose to sit in your study, sitting room, a park or your bedroom. Just make sure it is somewhere quiet so that you can think properly.

Step Three: Consider what you need to change about your organizing

Take a minute to think about the things bleeding for your attention. What are those objects or activities you would be glad to get rid of at the moment? Write those down in your journal. What is the state of your home, your health, your relationships, and your life in general?

Write those down. Are there friendships you need to declutter? Write those down.

Step Four: Set your decluttering goals.

Now that you know what you don't want whether it is the plates in the dishwasher, a friendship that is toxic or an overflowing inbox, think about what getting rid of those would do for you. Are there any specific advantages decluttering will bring you? Write those down. Make sure you write at least five ways that decluttering will make your life better. These are your decluttering goals.

Step Five: Keep your decluttering goals handy.

Do not allow the journal with your decluttering goals to get enmeshed in the clutter you are trying to get rid of in the first place. Keep it where you can easily see it when you need it.

Step Six: Visit your decluttering goals from time to time.

When you feel overwhelmed and lack the drive to continue decluttering, pick up your journal and read what you are trying to achieve. This way you will remain on track.

ACTIVITY TWO: WHAT IS POSSESSION SELF EXTENSION?

Set another time within the same day to practice the second activity. This activity will help you with your day two guide on getting organized in the next seven days. So it is important you carry out the activity before the day is over.

Step One: Reflect on everything you own with your journal and pen close by

Close your eyes while sitting or standing, whichever you prefer and try to mentally picture every single thing you own.

Step Two: Envision your sentimental clutter

Picture these objects again and think carefully about what each of them mean to you.

Step Three: Reflect

Think back of a time you gave something away. Was it hurtful? If it was, why do you think you were hurt about letting the item go?

Step Four: Envision your extended self in your possessions

Now picture the things you own again. Which of them will make you feel hurt if you should give them away? Why will you find it hard to let go of that item?

Step Five: Put it down

Now, open your eyes and sit if you were standing. Write down those things that you cannot part with.

Step Six: Decide whether or not you want to keep them

These possessions are your sentimental clutter and you view them as an extension of yourself. The pain that comes with letting them go is almost equal with that which comes from a physical blow. Choose if you want to walk yourself through this pain so that you are never attached to your possessions again or if you want to keep the objects.

Step Seven: Write down your decision

In front of each item, write down what you want to do with it.

Step Eight: Take action

If you want to let go of an item, close your eyes while you are seated and envision it again. Picture yourself in it and picture taking a scissors and cutting the items off you. Keep your list of items you want to let go of handy.

CHAPTER 6

WHEN IS THE RIGHT TIME
TO DEATH CLEAN?

As much as we condemn the consumerism culture of today, when you have lived a long and full life, owning too many things is not something that you can escape. Many of these things will carry memories of distant lives and distant lands for you. A time will come however when you will need to get rid of them. When exactly is this time?

There is no proper time for death cleaning. That sounds blank but it is the truth. The proper time for death cleaning is subjective; differing from person to person and so cannot be pinned down to a specific set of people.

This is what Magnusson means when she says a five year old can death clean. But she contradicts herself when she says that one should start death cleaning when one begins to think of death. However, if you did not start your decluttering earlier, you would have to start taking death cleaning seriously if you are beginning to think about death. When you begin to think that your last days are around the corner or when you begin to think about the frailty of life, you will need to start death cleaning. For some, this is around the age of sixty five but for others it is much later or much earlier.

Another way to determine when to start death cleaning is when the clutter around your life becomes overwhelming. Has your home become cramped because it is too small to contain your possessions? Then your death cleaning timing is around the corner. You can use the Swedish death cleaning concept to make your home tidier and to make your life run more smoothly.

Death cleaning is a continuous process. If you death clean once and forget about it, you will end up where you started. You death clean regularly, taking extra care to make it align with your goals. In the same manner, you should begin death cleaning early. This way it develops into a habit and the results are more pronounced in your everyday life.

IS THERE A PROPER WAY TO DEATH CLEAN?

We have been talking about the principles embedded in death cleaning for a while now. In this section, we are going to explore what these principles are. In reality, how do you go about death cleaning? The guiding principles of death cleaning could be summarized into four:

1. Approach death cleaning with a generous mind
2. Evaluate each of your possessions
3. Declutter
4. Have a practical method in place

So, death cleaning is about sorting out your life literarily.

CHAPTER 7

APPROACH DEATH CLEANING
WITH A GENEROUS MIND

This speaks of the attitude you should wear while you are death cleaning. Be open about it. Be thankful to have been able to use those items. Be thankful that now you have the opportunity to let them go and to allow them to be a blessing to someone else. Approach death cleaning with gratitude and with generosity.

EVALUATE EACH OF YOUR POSSESSIONS

This is the crux of death cleaning. Determine what to keep by considering whether or not each item would be a blessing to your loved ones after you are gone. Also, ask yourself if the item is fulfilling a need at the moment. Then decide to keep or remove the item based on your answers.

DECLUTTER

This is the next step in death cleaning where you do the actual organizing of your home. When following the principles of dostadning, you can either toss, donate or give out the items that you do not want to keep.

HAVE A PRACTICAL METHOD IN PLACE

You are to begin your death cleaning exercise from items you do not want or do not use and end it with your personal effects. This is because personal effects like photographs and journals have the ability to spark unwanted emotions that are capable of slowing you down. So, dostadning already has a practical method in place to help you achieve your death cleaning goals faster.

DAY TWO: EVALUATING YOUR POSSESSIONS

Today, you are to evaluate your possessions so that you know what you want to keep and what you want to toss. This would take you the entire day.

Step One: Get a big bag and wear an apron with a large pocket

Step Two: Start at your closet

Your clothes are the easiest things to declutter because you can acquire a large quantity and you can easily spot what you do not want.

Step Three: Hold each one and determine where it falls

Ask yourself the death cleaning questions as you hold each piece of clothing. 'Do I want this? 'What need does it serve?' 'Will my loved ones want it or will it burden them?

Step Four: Drop Clothes you do not want in the bag

Step Five: Repeat with all clothing and accessories

Step Six: Move to the kitchen, storage spaces, sitting room and do the same with all the items alternating between the bag and the apron to drop items. Then empty the items in the apron into the bag or into a different one if this bag is full.

Step Seven: End with your personal effects

By evening, you should be at your photographs and other personal items, drop in the bag those you want to toss and decide if you want to keep the rest of the photos or if you want to digitize them.

DAY THREE: YOUR BOOK OF PASSWORDS

Today, you are going to create your book of passwords.

Step One: Pick up a journal and a pen

Get a journal or a notebook and a pen. This journal should be different from the one you used in activity one and could be of aesthetic value if you like. It is a journal that is going to outlive you so preferably let it be empty.

Step Two: List your digital assets

Recollect all your on-line accounts including social media, amazon accounts, shopify and so on.

Step Three: Write down the login information

In front of each asset, write down your login information. This could be your username or an email address and your password to that account. Do not mix them up. Write each one carefully and correctly in front of its own account.

Step Four: List your financial assets

Do a separate list on a fresh page of all the financial institutions that you use. This should include both physical banks and on-line banks. Put down also any Internet banking platforms that you use.

Step Five: Write down the login information

Like before, write out opposite each institution any login information that you use.

Step Six: Visit your bank and update your information

Go over to your bank and update information about who should be able to access your accounts when you pass away. Update this information on your on-line bank accounts as well. Some on-line savings accounts have a provision for you to input your next of kin.

You can take this activity a step further by updating your social media handles and other digital assets as well. All you have to do is provide who you want to access them. You will see this feature in the legacy settings.

CHAPTER 8

SADNESS AND DEATH CLEANING

The natural reaction to death cleaning is to think that it is sad. Some people may even enter the actual exercise with this tendency towards sadness. But death cleaning is not sad. In fact, the actual translation of dostadning 'does not necessarily involve the dreaded fact of death; rather, it is the steady acknowledgment and anticipation that you should start shedding the baggage of life rather than leave it for your unfortunate children to deal with.' It is a stellar decluttering strategy that leaves your house sparkling with much needed space and therefore something you should be happy to participate in.

Death cleaning can be hard because it is a lot of work finding a purpose for each possession and then also decluttering but it is definitely not something to arouse sadness. In fact, the exercise ought to spark joy from reminiscing on a life lived well. This is why the attitude you approach death cleaning with is of enormous importance. You should be calm and joyful when you choose to death clean.

Death cleaning can ignite your negative emotions when you are depressed. So, that is not the time to go about it. Take your time to laugh at all the naughty things you have accumulated over the period that is your life.

DEALING WITH YOUR EMOTIONS

The frame of mind you enter death cleaning with is important to your initial emotional reaction to the process. Begin your death cleaning with a grateful heart and a tendency towards generosity. Engage in reflection within the time and celebrate your life's joys. Look at death cleaning from its kindness perspective. You are doing this in kindness to yourself and to your loved ones. When you view death cleaning like this, the thought of going through it and the thought of its results will leave you happy.

Also, during death cleaning itself, some of your possessions may spark feelings of nostalgia, pain or guilt. This is why dostadning suggests that you leave your personal effects until the end of the exercise. When you encounter this, you will need to walk yourself through the negative emotions and free yourself from them.

You might also experience feelings of attachment to some possessions but realizing that you do not have to own everything you love and admire will quickly walk you through this.

Death cleaning is an opportunity to come to terms with your emotions and to deal with them. Some of these emotions might have been in hiding for a long time. Looking at your life objectively can bring them to your glare and can also enable you to face them once and for all. You cannot effectively deal with your emotions if you do not first go through them. Thus, you should allow yourself to feel them no matter how negative they are. Cry if you want to but do not enter the next day of your death cleaning plan without first having gone through and dealt with that emotion.

MAKING DEATH CLEANING AN EMOTIONAL WORK OVER

One of the essential principles of Swedish death cleaning is involving others. You cannot properly death clean by going it alone. Consequently, you have to tell your family and your friends what you are doing. This quickly holds you accountable so that you complete the process. Communicate your intentions to your loved ones with a bright disposition. Don't give them the impression that you are about to die. That is not what death cleaning is about anyway. You can also use the death cleaning exercise as an avenue to open up discussions about death. This is especially important where your family has an elderly member. Death cleaning urges everyone and makes it easy to talk about death without fear.

Use the opportunity also to catch up with your friends. Invite them over and have everyone tell you what they would like to take from the items you do not want or do not use. However, keep away items you think everyone will want and give those to them as gifts instead. When death cleaning is happy, your negative emotions will no doubt be kept in check.

DAY FOUR: TURN DEATH CLEANING INTO A PARTY

Step One: Make a list of all your friends and loved ones that you want to be present as you death clean

Step Two: Pick up your phone and call every one of them to tell them you will be death cleaning

Step Three: Sit with your children and explain to them what you will be doing.

Listen to their concerns and answer their questions. This should be easy if they are adult children. For young children, you can simply explain that you will be organizing the house.

Step Four: Decide if you want a full blown party and prepare what your friends will take.

Your children can help you decide this.

Step Five: Remember the list you made in activity two about items you would love to let go of. Pick it up and carry every item on the list into the sitting room or the area you will be using for the exercise.

Step Six: Bring out also the bag that holds all the things you selected around the house as wanting to give away in day two

Step Seven: Spread out the items and let everyone present point to you what they want

Step Eight: Gather up the rest and label them as donations or gifts using boxes

Step Nine: Throw the rest away.

CHAPTER 9

EMOTIONAL CLUTTER

Many of us have some life event that we are still holding on to. Most of these events are negative and we might be holding on to them unconsciously. These events then build anger, pain and guilt within us; all of these emotions that are impeding our progress. These emotions are called your emotional clutter. They prevent you from being able to receive positive energy and from being able to connect to the things that mean the most to you.

Emotional clutter builds up because of disappointments, failures, rejection or challenges. Everyone experiences these and everyone has emotional clutter. The only difference is that some people let go of theirs.

The Swedish death cleaning exercise is a time for you to reflect on what types of emotional clutter might be holding you back. What is causing you to be so glued to the past when you should be setting goals for the future? What event caused that pain and hurt that you feel? You may have even tucked the clutter underneath other emotions but as you go through all of the items you own, you will encounter some that trigger the clutter all over again. Before your death cleaning plan is over, you should let go of these emotional baggage.

LETTING GO OF PAST HURTS

The ultimate way to let go of hurt is through forgiveness. You cannot trample on the pain until you have truly forgiven that person. When you are death cleaning, you are reflecting on your life and on life after you pass away. In this way, death cleaning has a tendency to open us up to depths of forgiveness. We more easily realize our own mortality and our tendency to hurt others as well.

So you need to practice two types of forgiveness. Forgive yourself and forgive others. When the photographs take you down memory lane, forgive what your spouse had done to you or what an ex had done.

You may also encounter your own failures and bad decisions. Something you ought to have done that you did not do or someone you ought to have helped that you did not help. Forgive yourself for not being able to do these things or for refusing to do them at the time. Do this consciously and free up the negativity. Call people you hold a grudge against to tell them you have forgiven them, if you can.

LETTING GO OF ATTACHMENT

The entire death cleaning concept is about letting go while you still can and not leaving that decision to other people to make for you. You have already identified in activity two of day one possessions that you are not willing to part with. You have also worked yourself through some of them but the rest you do not want to let go of. This is attachment. We are attached to our possessions because we see them as an extension of ourselves. In fact, a study by Roster and her colleagues through The Institute for Challenging Disorganization (ICD) on a sample of nearly 1500 adults aged 18 and older showed that these adults did not only see their possessions as an extension of themselves but were also attached to their homes. These objects that you are attached to but that take up space in your home are referred to as sentimental clutter. You are attached to them because you have given them some meaning and you relate some experiences to them. This is not a bad thing. As you death clean, you will both need to let go of attachment and to hold on to it. Items that have no meaning to anyone else but you, you will have to keep. Such items include things such as a dried up leaf that you admire, a hat from an escapade in Paris that is now out of fashion, shells that you picked by a waterside, gifts from your crushes in high school and so on.

All these items which hold value to you alone, you should keep. Put them in a box and label the box "throw away". This way, Swedish death cleaning allows you to enjoy them while you are still living and when you pass away, your loved ones will know to toss it out. If they do go through it, it will be with your permission.

For items that do not fall into this category and that you do not use but which you are attached to, you will need to walk through letting them go by showing yourself why you should. Allow them go and release any guilt you feel for giving them away. If you are elderly, decluttering sentimental clutter should not make you feel guilt. But if you are not, you are likely to feel that you will be offending the person or memory you attach to the item. Keep the memory but toss the object. Avoid the guilt trap because giving that object out to people who are more likely to make use of it does not mean that you have given the person or the memory behind them out as well. Look through those goals you listed in activity one and remind yourself why you must succeed at your decluttering and how organized your life will be afterwards.

DAY FIVE: PAVE WAY FOR ABUNDANCE

It is time for you to let go of everything that holds you back and by doing so open yourself to the abundance that the days ahead hold for you. Go through this activity with an open mind as always.

Step One: Pick the two boxes you labeled yesterday and place them in front of you.

These are your "donations" box and your "gifts" box.

Step Two: Taking each item, decide the appropriate places they should go.

This could include people or organizations

Step Three: Do a quick research on who can use the items

Research quickly using a computer, a mobile phone, a magazine, a journal and so on to see which organizations will be willing to collect which items.

Step Four: Call them

Pick up your phone and call the number provided to let them know you have some donations. Book an appointment with them to send the items over, to take them over by yourself or to have them come over to your house to pick up the items.

Step Five: Wave at the items as they go

If they do come to your house to pick them, give the items out with joy and wave at the truck as it leaves your yard

Step Six: Call the people

Call the people you have identified to come pick the items or take it over to them as presents. A good tip is giving out the items little by little when you have visitors or when you are a guest at your children's or grandchildren's or other loved ones' houses. You can use this tip to keep track of fresh accumulation.

CHAPTER 10

LIFE AFTER YOU DEATH CLEAN

Now, death cleaning isn't complete really if it is not continuous. You must have multiple 7 day death cleaning exercises to ensure that you do not slip back to where you were before you decided to declutter.

Also, you must take cognizance of your newly decluttered life and make lifestyle changes that fit this life. These changes differ from one person to another and from one age group to another. The elderly would be thinking of moving to a house that is smaller than the one in which they raised their children for example.

However, everyone death cleaning must put their wishes in a document that is easy to access. Hence, life after you death clean is futuristic. It is about creating newer joys for the rest of your life.

DOWNSIZING

This is the process by which elderly people declutter their homes.

Since all their children have left home, they can decide to move to a smaller apartment. Such small apartment will make it extremely easy for them to move around and it will also reduce any tendencies towards loneliness.

Now that you have decluttered all your belongings, a smaller place will fit perfectly. Your loved ones can come around to help you move the objects that you cannot move on your own or you can choose to use the services of move managers. Move managers will make the entire process seem very easy. Anyone who is in the process of selling their apartment will find decluttering valuable because having fewer possessions and hiding everything else away with storage boxes automatically makes the house worth more in the eyes of a buyer.

A cluttered apartment is upsetting and uninviting.

Documenting Your Wishes For The Rest of Your Possessions

After death cleaning, you will have items that you still want to use or that you still love. While you can enjoy them for as long as you want, they are the possessions that your loved ones will have to deal with at your passing. If you have specific people you will like to gift such items to, you should let these people know. But you do not have to tell them directly, you can document your wishes.

The same way you have kept a book of passwords, you can keep a book that contains your wishes as well. Who do you want to have what? What do you want to be done with what? All those should be written down in a book or a document made for that purpose.

One of the smartest ways to document your wishes and to make sure your estate runs more smoothly is to prepare a Will. Preparing a Will has enormous advantages for the kind of order it enforces in dealing with your possessions at your absence.

Also, it provides a framework for what ought to be done. This is one of the most important things you will leave behind. You can go about writing your Will yourself or you can employ the services of a solicitor. Solicitors charge a moderate price for documenting your wishes in your Will. Also, you can correct and review your Will from time to time using a Codicil, another document that your solicitor will prepare. It is advisable to review your Will every five years or after every major event of your life like getting married, having a child and so on. If you want to write your Will by yourself, there are on-line templates and guides on how to write one. You will need to know what your possessions are, who you want to give them to and who you want to enforce your Will. The person you entrust the performance of your Will onto is called your executor. If you are using a solicitor to prepare your Will, he will need all these information from you.

KEEPING TRACK OF FRESH ACCUMULATION

Death cleaning is incomplete if you go out there and begin acquiring newer possessions all over again. To deal with this, you must learn to differentiate between things you need and things you want.

Do not buy a new item unless you absolutely need it. Always learn to admire things without necessarily falling for the urge to buy them. If you want an organized home and life, it is absolutely important that you keep track of the newer things you acquire. Always take stock of the things you already own, removing those that you do not use frequently out of sight. Use storage boxes to store them away and to constantly keep a neat home. Arrange the rest of your possessions in such a way that you know where each item is located. This way you can easily go to the specific drawer when you need something and you will also have destroyed the urge to rush out and buy a new one. If you do get newer items, make it a regular duty to purge your home and keep it intact.

DAY SIX: PREPARE YOUR WILL

Step One: Pick up a journal and a pen

Yes, you need to do some writing again. Get your journal but not your book of passwords of course. Get a pen too.

Step Two: Find a quiet place to sit

This could be a park, your bedroom, your study or any other place.

Step Three: Reflect on all the things you own now

Step Four: Reflect on the people you would like to give them to

Step Five: Write these down

Put in writing the things you own and the people you will like to have them at your passing as you have identified in steps one and two

Step Six: Think of any trusted friend you will like to enforce this

Make this person your executor by writing down his or her name in your journal you can have one or two executors. The alternative executor helps out if the executor is unable to act.

Step Seven: Go find a solicitor or an on-line template

You may feel more secure getting a solicitor to do your Will or you may use free templates available on-line. Be careful to follow the template as instructed.

Step Eight: Keep your Will in a safe place

Often your loved ones and your executor should not find your Will until your passing. Keep it in a safe but easy to find location. Alternatively, hand it to your solicitor for safe keeping.

CHAPTER 11

PRACTISING ESSENTIALISM

There is a very eye-opening concept for me that I will like to share here. It is called essentialism. It is an idea outlined by Greg McKeown in his book, Essentialism: The Disciplined Pursuit of Doing Less. The concept postulates that we should take on less tasks in order to achieve more. Essentialism points to societal beliefs that we must do more work until we attain our glorious success. This success is viewed as career advancement and wealth. Essentialism however says that the more things we do, the less we will achieve. Essentialists believe that more work only results in stress. Also, the most important things in life and the true measure of success is not our wealth or career success but our health, our family and our general wellbeing. Essentialism says that any work that is not targeted towards or inclusive of these is not worthy of our attention. Hence, to become an essentialist, you must know when you are drowning in tasks and learn to say no to more. You must be disciplined enough to take on only tasks that align with your goals. This takes a high level of selectiveness because you have to look at proposals with scrutiny before you accept them. Also, you have to know how much you can carry on at particular times and you also have to be disciplined enough not to cross that limit.

One of the beautiful principles of essentialism is that you should take more time to plan. Greg believes that getting things done usually take longer than we often budget. To enable you not to get overwhelmed by work, therefore, you must include additional time within which to carry out each task. Essentialism opposes the endowment effect and explains that we do not have to own an object in order for us to value it. This principle is at the heart of death cleaning. Attaching the value that objects possess to the fact of ownership will keep us attached to them. We have to let go of such attachment to properly declutter and we also have to refrain from buying everything that we admire. To keep on top of your death cleaning and not return to a life of clutter therefore, you have to become an essentialist. Essentialism will help keep your life organized because you will feel mentally decluttered and emotionally decluttered. You will know that not all meetings deserve your attention and you will be able to miss out without guilt so that you can attend to the tasks you have at hand and not keep deadlines nudging at you endlessly.

CONCLUSION

Now that you have the top key simple steps to Swedish death cleaning. You don't worry if you are not close to your retirement, but once you are suffering from poverty, it will hit you hard.

Don't make the same old mistakes by procrastinating what you don't like.

Going through a family members stuff is heartbreaking. Save your family from this awful process.

Practice these steps daily and use these new tracks you discover to help make daily choices on what you bring home.

Welcome to your new minimalistic lifestyle.

CPSIA information can be obtained
at www.ICGtesting.com
Printed in the USA
LVHW010028160723
752584LV00037B/445